EDUCATE. MOTIVATE. ILLUMINATE.

"

I Will...

A 30 Day Devotional Journal of Self Reflection and Transparency

TERRI MATTHEWS

"

30 Days of I Will

I WILL...

A 30 Day Devotional Journal of Self Reflection and Transparency

Copyright © 2018 by Terri Matthews
www.terrimatthewsonline.com

No Part of this work may be reproduced without the written permission from the Publisher.

All rights reserved.

ISBN: 1720133247

ISBN-13: 9781720133247

30 Days of I Will

DEDICATION

This devotional is dedicated to my husband, my children, my family, my vision partners and the people I have met along my life's journey. Each one has helped shape, develop and encourage me. My trials have pushed me past simply existing, to learning, living and giving so that I can continue to pour out more love.

30 Days of I Will

Table of Contents:

ACKNOWLEDGMENTS	9
WHY I WILL	10
YOUR WORDS HAVE POWER	14
THE REASON FOR 30 DAYS	15
WHAT TO EXPECT	17
START YOUR JOURNEY	19

30 Days of I Will

ACKNOWLEDGMENTS

There are people who helped birth this book that I want to thank:

My Lord and Savior, Jesus Christ
Charo J. who keeps me seeing life from a different lens.
LaQuanda M. who participates in the path of my destiny.
My Family and friends who pray for me and remind me all things are possible. My vision partners aka my Dream Team who carry me so I don't fall. My enemies because even Jesus used Judas to fulfill the promise.

30 Days of I Will

WHY I WILL

By the age of 18 years old, I was a single mother to one of the most beautiful human beings I've ever met. I didn't have a lot of parental support during that time because my parents were battling their own demons, so I learned early on how to fend for myself. Life had stacked some pretty unfair obstacles against me and I dealt with molestation, homelessness, abuse – you name it. During all the turmoil in my life, I learned resiliency from my grandfather. His lessons showed me that I was strong enough to withstand whatever came my way, and because of those lessons, I adopted an I can mentality around 10 or 11 years old. It started with my saying simple phrases like, I can handle this or I can overcome that. In my eyes, life forced me to become my own super hero and the S I wore on my chest was the scripture, Philippians 4:13, "I can do all things through Christ who strengthens me."

I went on to tackle life, becoming a successful business woman, mother and wife. But still in my life of I cans, I felt this internal longing to go further and to do more, so, I began to write out a long list of things I envisioned, and that God showed me. I was very excited about writing out the vision because that meant I tackled the first part of the process as instructed in Habakkuk 2:2, "Write the vision, and make it plain."

When I periodically went back to read the items on my list, I noticed that the completion box next to many of the items was left unchecked. In trying to figure out why I wasn't getting the things on my list done, I recognized it wasn't because I lacked the ability to complete them. I knew I could do them, and so the question became, why wasn't I? As always, life pushed on and different circumstances and my own excuses kept me from taking a closer look at why I wasn't completing certain God assigned tasks in my life and before I knew it, years had gone by. I grew tired and frustrated with my incomplete list, so I sought after God with my why and that's when God really got my attention and forced me to make a monumental shift that wrecked my world completely. He revealed that His vision for my life superseded all I could do on my own strength, knowledge and ability.

30 Days of I Will

God began to challenge everything I knew about myself. I discovered two very important things about myself and the I can mentality. The first thing was that I can didn't demand any follow through. It was simply a proclamation of one's own ability. And secondly, as much as I thought I was leaning and depending on God, I can didn't require me to trust God at all. I realized that I'd reduced God to what I could accomplish with my own resources and capacity. I had no faith outside of what I could make happen on my own, and if I was going to accomplish the things that God showed me and that I wrote down on that list, I would have to shift the narrative completely.

I had to change my language from I can to I will because I will goes beyond a proclamation of ability. This simple, yet incredibly powerful shift in words, challenged me because it signified a supporting action immediately following my declaration. I will became the directive that propelled me into action.

After that revelation, I quickly made the changes from I will to I WILL, which still is my bold response to God when He challenges me to grow up in my faith and to accept and execute His vision for my life on His terms. God knows I can write a check and I have and will write plenty more of them. But when God says, "sell everything you have because I have a different plan for your life" or "take your children and move to a place where you don't know anybody" my response to God is still I WILL. Now, it isn't always easy to comply with these kinds of requests from God, but I surrendered my will to His and he has blessed me exponentially because of my obedience.

Often, there are things God is calling us to do and, because we've been taught scriptures like Phillipians 4:13, I can do all things through Christ who strengthens me, we acknowledge in God that we can do incredible things, but the real questions are will we and do we even trust God at all?

The question I have for you reading this journal is, will you? Will you heal? Will you pray? Will you be obedient? Will you answer the call?

30 Days of I Will

Understand, God created us all with a purpose. He has a call on every one of our lives. He's allowed certain situations to arise that challenge us and grow us and he's given us the Holy Spirit to have the ability to do all things, if we WILL. Whenever you feel weakened or defeated, it's important you understand that you are not alone in taking action. The Holy Spirit is your partner in execution because it's not possible to do an I WILL without God.

Let God speak to your heart as you work through this journal. Let Him deliver his direction for your life directly to you. This may seem new and unfamiliar but it's a fairly simple process and you start by just being honest with yourself. Be transparent about what you think and feel. God doesn't want us to remain the same. We are walking billboards for him with different experiences that collectively come together for the greater purpose. I know it takes a while to get there.

Think of this journal as the start. It's a way to start looking at real places in your life where you can actually make change. You have to start with your foundation and unearth some hurt, so you can build something that withstands the test of time and the trials that are sure to come. Sometimes, when people want to heal, they can't because they can't be honest with themselves. Nobody wants to admit they're still hurting because of an ex or they're still dealing with bitterness from childhood trauma and rejection. Everybody wants to look good on the outside, like they have it all together, but that's just not true for everyone. We all have fears. We all struggle. Your kids really do get on your nerves. Whatever it is, it's about being honest with yourself and honesty requires doing some digging and that digging has to be done in a safe space.

This journal is your safe space. This is where you start to repair the broken places. This is where you start excavating the dirt to make sure your ground is level, so what you're building won't sink. God teaches us not to build our houses on sinking sand, but you must understand that you are the foundation of whatever you build. If the dirt isn't right, you've got a problem. You can't even pour concrete unless the ground is good. You must be excavated. You have got to be cleaned out.

30 Days of I Will

Think about anytime someone builds a house. The longest period is spent on the foundation. Once the foundation is right, the walls go up in 30 days or so. Everything moves quickly once the foundation is laid. Until then, you'll be looking at the ground and wondering when they're going to start working. Sometimes, it looks like they're just shoveling and moving dirt around and then you start to question the process. Still, even though you can't see the finished work, understand that through every phase of this process God is moving things around for your good.

The fear that most people have is of time. "If I take the time to work on me or if I take the time to do all these things, it's going to take me so much longer to execute my dream." But, if you go ahead and build anything, without the ground being on solid foundation, it will crack, it will lean and it will crumble under pressure.

You are digging to find out more about you so can lay your sure foundation. Saying, I will and I WILL, is a part of your excavation process. It allows you to remove damaged things from your life, so you can pour only what's necessary into your foundation. During this process you will come across some rocky areas in your past, places where you just buried the hurt and kept going. There will be obstacles, but that does not give you the green light to stop digging. It means you must acknowledge these are the cracks or the concerns that could ruin your foundation. If you don't get your thoughts, your heart, your mind around what those things are, sure you can go ahead and build if you want to, but at the end, somewhere within your building, what you didn't excavate, and what you didn't deal with shoveling, moving out the way or acknowledging, will manifest itself somewhere else in what you're building.

Saying, I WILL is like pouring the right substances into your foundation. It's acknowledging that you don't have to build your life out of brokenness. You don't have to build your life out of pain and don't have to build your life out of shame. Use your I WILLS to help build your foundation. Set them as the building blocks for your life's vision. Write them down as instructed by God in Habakkuk 2:2.

YOUR WORDS HAVE POWER
"Change your words, change your world"

I am a firm believer that we possess the power with our words to influence and heal ourselves. I can boldly affirm that statement because I have personally witnessed the powerful impact affirming words had in my spiritual, personal and professional life. God, in His Word also warns us to be careful of what we say, how we say it and when we say it. I'm sure there are plenty of scriptures out there, but these come to mind as even today I remind myself of the importance of words:

- Proverbs 18:21 ESV
  "Death and life are in the power of the tongue, and those who love it will eat its fruits."

- Ephesians 4:29 ESV
  "Let no corrupting talk come out of your mouths, but only such as is good for building up, as fits the occasion, that it may give grace to those who hear."

30 Days of I Will

THE REASON FOR 30 DAYS

The reason I chose the 30-day format was because of the biblical significance of the number. I wanted to share some powerful examples of the number 30 to encourage your completion of this devotional.

- Joseph was 30 years old when he became second in command to Pharaoh, after being in prison as a slave in Egypt. "And Joseph was thirty years old when he stood before Pharaoh king of Egypt. And Joseph went out from the presence of Pharaoh, and went throughout all the land of Egypt." (Genesis 41:46 MSG)

- The priests officially entered service at age 30. "From thirty years old and upward even until fifty years old, all that enter into the host, to do the work in the tabernacle of the congregation." (Numbers 4:3)

- When Moses died, the Israelites mourned him for 30 days. "And the children of Israel wept for Moses in the plains of Moab thirty days: so, the days of weeping and mourning for Moses were ended." (Deuteronomy 34:8)

- David became King when he was 30 years old. He was a mere Shepard before his anointing. "David was thirty years old when he began to reign, and he reigned forty years." (2 Samuel 5:4)

- Ezekiel was called by God as a prophet at age 30. "Now it came to pass in the thirtieth year, in the fourth month, in the fifth day of the month, as I was among the captives by the river of Chebar, that the heavens were opened, and I saw visions of God." (Ezekiel 1:1)

- John the Baptist was age 30 when he came out from the wilderness to pave the way for the Messiah (Jesus). We know John was roughly 30 because the Bible says he was born 6 months before Jesus, and Jesus started his ministry at age 30.

- Jesus officially started his ministry at age 30. Before this time, he worked as a carpenter. "Now Jesus himself was about thirty years old when he began his ministry. He was the son, so it was thought, of Joseph (Luke 3:23)"

- Judas betrayed Jesus for 30 pieces of silver. "Then one of the twelve, named Judas Iscariot, went to the chief priests and said, "What are you willing to give me to betray Him to you?" And they weighed out thirty pieces of silver to him. From then on he began looking for a good opportunity to betray Jesus." (Matthew 26:14)

30 Days of I Will

WHAT TO EXPECT

This journal will take you on a journey of self-discovery. I must warn you that this process will only work if you do. It will challenge you to be authentic, transparent, honest and accountable so that you can rise to the best version of yourself. You must have the courage to dig within yourself, be accountable to yourself and be willing to listen to yourself to get the results intended.

Once you complete this journal, I challenge you to use it as a reminder to focus less on the problems and more on the promises. Use the words to increase your faith, strengthen your heart, and walk in your purpose. Use these words to encourage yourself and be your own cheerleader, warrior and doer.

AFTER YOU'VE FINISHED

Once completed this IWILL Devotional Journal will become a tool for you to use when life gets busy and challenging. If you lose focus this tool WILL get you back on track by reviewing the words you have written for yourself. Use it to remind you, encourage you, develop you as a leader, increase your Faith, and teach you to trust the process even when you don't understand the plan.

START YOUR

JOURNEY

> I Will...
>
> BEGIN

Day 1

Eliminate the excuses and begin Loving, Living, Learning, Doing, Giving, Hoping, Believing, Working, Listening and Laughing. Don't allow fear to intimidate you from beginning.

What **Will** you **BEGIN** doing today?

"

*Have I not commanded you? Be strong and courageous!
Do not be terrified or dismayed (intimidated), for the
Lord your God is with you wherever you go.*

- Joshua 1:9 AMP -

"

" I Will... PRAY "

Day 2

I wasn't always consistent in prayer until I realized that prayer was simply an easy going, under-complicated conversation with God. Whether romantic, professional or spiritual, the foundation of any successful relationship is built on communication. If you want your romantic relationship enhanced, start talking to each other. You want your professional relationship improved? Open the lines of communication. You want your relationship with God enriched? Pray.

What commitment **Will** you make to **PRAYER**?

> *For this reason I am telling you, whatever things you ask for in prayer [in accordance with God's will], believe [with confident trust] that you have received them, and they will be given to you.*
>
> *- Mark 11:24 AMP -*

> # I Will...
>
> # FORGIVE

Day 3

Forgiveness is an essential component of your growth and healing even in the absence of an apology. I had to learn to first forgive myself and others no matter how hurt I was or how unfair it seemed. Forgiveness doesn't mean you are forgetting or excusing the inflicted harm. Forgiveness means you will not allow bitterness, anger and any other emotion associated with unforgiveness to hold you hostage to the past or rob you of your peace.

How and what **Will** you **FORGIVE** today?

> Be kind and helpful to one another, tender-hearted [compassionate, understanding], forgiving one another [readily and freely], just as God in Christ also forgave you.
>
> - *Ephesians 4:32 AMP* -

> # I Will...
> # LOVE

Day 4

Love is one of the most powerful emotions and the greatest commandment from God. Truth be told, I experienced so many challenges in life that I thought love was unattainable. If the people that were supposed to love me the most let me down then how could I believe that true love was available? So, I loved but the love I had was anchored in fear and was limited because love had failed me. Once I discovered that I was created in the image of God who is Love and that God loves me completely, I had the freedom to love beyond my hurt, and to love beyond the pain that limited my capacity to love freely. I started to love myself and reshape my perspective of what love is.

How **Will** you begin to **LOVE** yourself today?

Love bears all things [regardless of what comes], believes all things [looking for the best in each one], hopes all things [remaining steadfast during difficult times], endures all things [without weakening].

- 1 Corinthians 13:7 AMP -

> # I Will...
> # GIVE

Day 5

I didn't learn to give because someone taught to me in church or by reading the bible, although God does teach us about giving in His Word. I learned to give because of the countless occasions when I needed someone to give to me. Sometimes their gift was much-needed shelter, food or opportunity. The impact of their giving is one that I will never forget. It is with that same sentiment that I make giving to others a priority. My gift could very well be a lifeline to someone in need.

What **Will** you begin to **GIVE** today?

_____
_____
_____
_____
_____
_____
_____
_____
_____
_____
_____
_____
_____
_____
_____
_____
_____
_____

The generous man [is a source of blessing and] shall be prosperous and enriched, and he who waters will himself be watered [reaping the generosity he has sown].

- Proverbs 11:25 AMP -

> # I Will...
>
> # ADJUST

Day 6

Every change, challenge, or storm in life has the ability to shake us or shape us. Regardless of its intent, how you adjust, determines your outcome. If a caterpillar didn't adjust to living in a cocoon it would never be able to become a butterfly. I learned to adjust to the challenges in my life so they didn't become a hindrance rather a catalyst for my future.

How and what Will you ADJUST?

_____
_____
_____
_____
_____
_____
_____
_____
_____
_____
_____
_____
_____
_____
_____

> Do not be anxious or worried about anything,
> but in everything [every circumstance and situation]
> by prayer and petition with thanksgiving, continue to
> make your [specific] requests known to God. 7 And the
> peace of God [that peace which reassures the heart,
> that peace] which transcends all understanding,
> [that peace which] stands guard over your hearts and
> your minds in Christ Jesus [is yours]
>
> *- Philippians 4: 6-7 AMP -*

> "I Will... BELIEVE"

Day 7

As a serial entrepreneur, the number one thing I had to learn is that my confidence is a direct result of what I believe. If I didn't believe it could happen who else would I be able to convince. My success started with me believing success was possible for me.

What **Will** you begin to **BELIEVE** today?

_____
_____
_____
_____
_____
_____
_____
_____
_____
_____
_____
_____
_____
_____
_____
_____
_____
_____

Now faith is the assurance (title deed, confirmation) of things hoped for (divinely guaranteed), and the evidence of things not seen [the conviction of their reality--faith comprehends as fact what cannot be experienced by the physical senses].

- Hebrews 11:1 AMP -

" I Will...

HOPE "

Day 8

I had quite a few let downs in life that could have had a permanent negative impact on my thoughts. I was determined not to allow those let downs to suffocate my expectations. Hope, at times, was all I had to get me through the next moment in life and it is still what I lean on today.

What **Will** you **HOPE** for?

May the God of hope fill you with all joy and peace in believing [through the experience of your faith] that by the power of the Holy Spirit you will abound in hope and overflow with confidence in His promises.

- Romans 15:13 AMP -

"I Will...

TRUST"

Day 9

If you believe in God and you know He created you, you can trust that he has equipped you with all you need to live a full life? Trust the process, yourself and the outcome.

How **Will** you learn to **TRUST** yourself?

___

> *Trust in and rely confidently on the LORD with all your heart And do not rely on your own insight or understanding. In all your ways know and acknowledge and recognize Him, And He will make your paths straight and smooth [removing obstacles that block your way].*
>
> *- Proverbs 3:5-6 AMP -*

> # I Will...
>
> # RELEASE

Day 10

I had to let go of every thought that limited my capacity to see beyond where I was. Honestly speaking, it isn't easy because challenges are real and life is real. Letting go is a daily process in order to eliminate stagnation from your life.

What **Will** you **RELEASE** today to be set free?

> *Brothers and sisters, I do not consider that I have made it my own yet; but one thing I do: forgetting what lies behind and reaching forward to what lies ahead, I press on toward the goal to win the [heavenly] prize of the upward call of God in Christ Jesus*
>
> *- Philipians 3:13-14 AMP -*

" I Will...

ACKNOWLEDGE "

Day 11

I had to learn to acknowledge my successes the same way I acknowledge my mistakes. It's okay to pat yourself on the back sometimes. Acknowledging your growth doesn't make you conceited or cocky. In fact, healthy applause will produce Godly confidence, promote healing, increase your faith and give you the courage you need to climb the next mountain in your life.

What **Will** you **ACKNOWLEDGE** today?

_____

_____

_____

_____

_____

_____

_____

_____

_____

_____

_____

_____

_____

_____

_____

"

*I can do all things [which He has called me to do]
through Him who strengthens and empowers me
[to fulfill His purpose—I am self-sufficient in Christ's
sufficiency; I am ready for anything and equal to
anything through Him who infuses me with inner
strength and confident peace.]*

- Philipians 4:13 AMP -

"

> # I Will...
> # EMBRACE

Day 12

I learned to have a healthy mix of embracing people, possibility and change. This allowed me to be fluid and flexible in life which produced amazing opportunities for me to grow.

What **Will** you start to **EMBRACE**?

> *Be assured that the testing of your faith [through experience] produces endurance [leading to spiritual maturity, and inner peace]. And let endurance have its perfect result and do a thorough work, so that you may be perfect and completely developed [in your faith], lacking in nothing*
>
> - *James 1:3-4 AMP* -

" I Will...

CHANGE "

Day 13

A change had to occur for me from the inside out. There were habits, mindsets and attitudes I adopted that were counter-intuitive to the direction God purposed for my life. I had to be honest with myself about my flaws and come to terms with the things that required a change in order to embrace my God-given purpose. Once I was able to handle my change, I became an example for others, encouraging them to know that if I can change after everything I've experienced then change was possible for them.

What **Will** you **CHANGE** for a better tomorrow?

There is a season (a time appointed) for everything and a time for every delight and event or purpose under heaven

- Ecclesiastes 3:1 AMP -

"I Will... PURSUE"

Day 14

The life-changing question for me was did I pursue my self-improvement in the same manner I pursued business and other opportunities? Did I pursue changing negative thoughts, attitudes and actions. Did I pursue a healthy relationship with God? Was I loving myself correctly? After taking serious inventory, I realized that sustaining a successful business or maintaining great relationships required me to pursue a healthier version of myself.

What **Will** you **PURSUE** about yourself today to live a better tomorrow?

_____

_____

_____

_____

_____

_____

_____

_____

_____

_____

_____

_____

_____

_____

_____

_____

> *So then, let us pursue [with enthusiasm] the things which make for peace and the building up of one another [things which lead to spiritual growth].*
>
> *- Romans 14:19 AMP -*

> "I Will... COMPLETE"

Day 15

Don't look at how big or small something is or even measure the significance of what you are working on to justify if you should finish it or not. Finishing is necessary because it builds confidence, position and character. Even the times when I wanted to give up, I was reminded that God gave me a vision, not to frustrate me but for me to complete it.

What **Will** you **FINISH** today?

> *I am convinced and confident of this very thing, that He who has begun a good work in you will [continue to] perfect and complete it until the day of Christ Jesus [the time of His return].*
>
> *- Philippians 1:6 AMP -*

> # I Will...
>
> # PERSEVERE

Day 16

It's not by accident that you survived it, that, them. You survived for a reason, keep going!

List things you have persevered through and **Will** you **PERSERVERE** today?

_____
_____
_____
_____
_____
_____
_____
_____
_____
_____
_____
_____
_____
_____
_____
_____
_____
_____
_____

> *You survived it... that, them, they for a reason, keep going." TM "Blessed [happy, spiritually prosperous, favored by God] is the man who is steadfast under trial and perseveres when tempted; for when he has passed the test and been approved, he will receive the [victor's] crown of life which the Lord has promised to those who love Him.*
>
> *- James 1:12 AMP -*

" I Will...

PROTECT "

Day 17

Protecting my thoughts and who entered my space was important for me to be successful. Whoever and whatever occupies our space could greatly influence our atmosphere. We are a product of our thoughts and our social circles.

How **Will** you **PROTECT** yourself today?

> *No weapon that is formed against you will succeed; And every tongue that rises against you in judgment you will condemn. This [peace, righteousness, security, and triumph over opposition] is the heritage of the servants of the LORD, and this is their vindication from Me," says the LORD.*
>
> *- Isaiah 54:17 AMP -*

> # I Will...
>
> # ENOURAGE

Day 18

I am stronger because I had to be. I am smarter because of my mistakes. I love because I know what not being loved feels like. I am wiser because I have learned from all these experiences. There are a million things that can bring you down find the reason to bring you up.

How **Will** you **ENCOURAGE** yourself today?

> *Therefore encourage and comfort one another and build up one another, just as you are doing.*
>
> *- 1 Thessalonians 5:11 AMP -*

> # I Will...
> # OVERCOME

Day 19

My struggles came in all shapes and sizes. I later realized that my struggles were part of my personal test of growth. God does not tempt us but he allows us to go through so we can grow through. When we overcome it gives us strength, endurance and Godly confidence to walk over every mountain and/or obstacle in our lives or command them to move.

What have you **OVERCOME** and what **Will** you **OVERCOME**?

> *Do not be overcome and conquered by evil, but overcome evil with good.*
>
> *- Romans 12:21 AMP -*

"I Will...

LISTEN"

Day 20

We have two ears and one mouth for a reason. It's for us to listen more than we speak. Sometimes we spend so much time talking that we don't hear the instructions for the next phase of our lives. We can't talk and tune in to God at the same time.

How **Will** you **LISTEN** to God?

_____
_____
_____
_____
_____
_____
_____
_____
_____
_____
_____
_____
_____
_____
_____
_____
_____
_____

> *Listen carefully and hear the words of the wise, and apply your mind to my knowledge;*
>
> *- Proverbs 22:17 AMP -*

> # I Will...
> # GROW

Day 21

God changes caterpillars into butterflies, sand into pearls and coal into diamonds using both pressure and time. Trust the process even when you don't understand the plan.

What **Will** you do, allow and work on so to can **GROW**?

> *For I know the plans and thoughts that I have for you,' says the Lord, 'plans for peace and well-being and not for disaster, to give you a future and a hope.*
>
> *- Jeremiah 29:11 AMP -*

> # I Will...
>
> # LEARN

Day 22

God makes no mistakes. Everything in life happens with intention; even painful moments can be teachable moments with the right perspective. Training is required for the perfecting of our gifts. What we may consider pain could very well be the training ground for our purpose. Some of our training will require us to go back to school, find a mentor, read books or experience hardships. Whatever your process requires, learn from it.

What **Will** you do to **LEARN** more about your gift or calling today?

> *And we know [with great confidence] that God [who is deeply concerned about us] causes all things to work together [as a plan] for good for those who love God, to those who are called according to His plan and purpose.*
>
> *- Romans 8:28 AMP -*

"I Will...
SOW"

Day 23

Before reaping the benefits of anything there must be labor. Whatever you plant (sow) is what you will see (reap) in your life. If you sow seeds of negative attitudes, finances and behaviors, that's exactly what you'll receive. There is a saying, "you want better, you do better". I say to you, if you want a harvest, sow with the expectation of receiving one.

How **Will** you **SOW** today?

> *Now [remember] this: he who sows sparingly will also reap sparingly, and he who sows generously [that blessings may come to others] will also reap generously [and be blessed].*
>
> *- 2 Corinthians 9:6 AMP -*

> # I Will...
> # LAUGH

Day 24

Laugh at yourself, your mistakes, your challenges, your obstacles and your pain. All of those things will wind up working out for your good. Life can be very heavy at times but you have to find reasons to smile and do it often because laughter is good for the soul.

What **Will** you **LAUGH** at today?

And we know [with great confidence] that God [who is deeply concerned about us] causes all things to work together [as a plan] for good for those who love God, to those who are called according to His plan and purpose

- Romans 8:28 AMP -

> # I Will...
>
> # REST

Day 25

Learning to rest is most challenging for me. My mind and my body are constantly in motion. However, I have learned the importance of slowing things down. I can't out work God. I can't move faster than what He has ordained. I can't avoid the process He requires for my growth. Rest is essential in order to regroup, adjust, gain strength and to move forward.

What **Will** you **REST** from?

> *Let us therefore make every effort to enter that rest [of God, to know and experience it for ourselves], so that no one will fall by following the same example of disobedience [as those who died in the wilderness].*
>
> *- Hebrews 4:11 AMP -*

"I Will...

LEAD"

Day 26

Leaders are not merely positions or titles. Leadership is a responsibility to guide, support, train, develop and nurture people. It should not be a position where you bark out demands and orders simply because you are the person in power. Great leadership starts with servanthood. Great leaders are concerned about the well-being of the people they are leading.

How **Will** you learn to **LEAD** today?

_____
_____
_____
_____
_____
_____
_____
_____
_____
_____
_____
_____
_____
_____
_____
_____
_____

> *Do nothing from selfishness or empty conceit [through factional motives, or strife], but with [an attitude of] humility [being neither arrogant nor self-righteous], regard others as more important than yourselves.*
>
> *- Philippians 2:3 AMP -*

"
I Will...

HEAL
"

Day 27

God desires the healing of brokenness. The term brokenness denotes a full range of conditions, including, emotional, physical, spiritual, social and psychological issues. These create barriers to the receipt and appropriation of divine grace. Healing from past hurts plays a huge part in your personal growth. I've learned not to carry emotional baggage that isn't meant for me to lug around because the weight was too heavy for me. I had to learn to let it go through prayer and wise counsel.

What **Will** you **HEAL** from today?

> *He sent His word and healed them, and rescued them from their destruction.*
>
> *- Psalm 107:20 AMP -*

"I Will...

PROSPER "

Day 28

Coming from modest beginnings my perception of prosperity was skewed. I thought having lots of money equated to prosperity and the exodus from poverty. During that time, I failed to realize that poverty is a mindset and prosperity applies to anything that experiences growth and success. I learned the hard way not to chase money, love or success. But in becoming the best version of myself, all those things will begin to chase after me!

What areas **Will** you **PROSPER** in?

> *The LORD will open for you His good treasure house, the heavens, to give rain to your land in its season and to bless all the work of your hand; and you will lend to many nations, but you will not borrow.*
>
> *- Deuteronomy 28:12 AMP -*

"I Will...
PLAN"

Day 29

Procrastination and preparation are both intentional. We spend substantial amounts of our lifespan either planning to waste or planning to win. Wasting didn't work well for me because I wanted to be everything God showed me I would be, so I started planning for the WIN! When I planned for the win, I started winning... it wasn't easy and wasn't instant. There were plenty of days I didn't feel like executing my plans but I had to remind myself that I'm a winner, not a waster.

What **Will** you **PLAN** and execute today?

> *The plans of the diligent lead to profit as surely as haste leads to poverty.*
>
> *- Proverbs 21:5 AMP -*

"I Will...

END"

Day 30

It was important for me to close some doors (END) in my life that tore me down, stagnated my movement, decreased my growth, developed fear, created unhealthy relationships, encouraged me to forget my dreams and blurred my vision. ALL of these things attempted to keep me from reaching my destiny and I don't want that to happen to you! In order to create new beginnings, we have to be brave enough to bring some old things to an end.

What behaviors, attitudes, relationships **Will** you **END** today?

> *There is a season (a time appointed) for everything and a time for every delight and event or purpose under heaven...*
>
> *- Ecclesiastes 3:1 AMP -*

Made in the USA
Columbia, SC
13 May 2024